D0771161

FLORIDA

A PICTURE BOOK TO REMEMBER HER BY

Designed by
DAVID GIBBON

Produced by
TED SMART

CRESCENT

INTRODUCTION

Twenty years after he is believed to have sailed with Columbus, the Spanish soldier and explorer Ponce de Leon first sighted the coast of Florida. The year was 1513 and on the 3rd of April, Easter Day, he landed at St Augustine, claiming the country for Spain. He returned to his homeland a few months later to announce the discovery of what he had taken to be an island, and was given permission by King Ferdinand to colonize it.

When he returned he attempted to start a colony on the west coast but it was to last for only six months and Ponce de Leon, during a skirmish in the struggle to survive, received a severe arrow-wound, of which he was to die in Cuba. For over 200 years, however, Spain remained in control of Florida, despite intermittent warfare against the English and the French, who were both eager to gain a foothold in this part of the continent.

In 1763 Florida was ceded to England by a treaty of Paris – only to be reclaimed by Spain twenty years later. Eventually, in 1819, the United States purchased the land for five million dollars and in 1845 it became a State of the Union. Nevertheless, the fighting that had been going on for over 300 years was not at an end and the Seminole Wars began – seven long years of bitter struggle. The reason for these wars was simply that President Andrew Jackson signed a law – the Indian Removal Bill – whereby all tribes of Red Indians living east of the Mississippi River were to cede their land in exchange for territory in the west.

One tribe refused to move. In Florida the Seminoles resisted the Bill and from the protection of the swampy Everglades Chief Os-ce-o-la and between three and four thousand braves waged a guerilla war. Seminole women even killed their children in order to be free to fight alongside their men.

After seven relentless years the fighting ended, when the last important leader of the tribe, Billy Bowlegs, and his followers were sent west. Even so, a small number of Seminoles chose to remain in the Everglades, where some of their descendants live to this day, carrying on their traditional way of life. As a peace treaty with the government was never implemented they remain, technically, at war with the United States.

The publicity that resulted from the Seminole Wars encouraged pioneers to settle in this southern peninsula but Florida's real development came about in the 1880's. Two of the wealthiest men in the state, Henry M. Flagler and H.B. Plant, recognized the area's potential and built railroads and hotels which signalled the commencement of tourism.

A real estate boom followed but, in 1926, just before the Great Depression, this came to an end and fortunes were lost overnight. In order to help prevent another disaster of such proportions controlled planning was introduced, particularly in the areas of agriculture, industry and tourism and this has resulted in Florida having one of the highest standards of living in the whole of America.

Where farming is concerned the state is world famous for the production of citrus fruits – especially oranges and grapefruits – and for the growing of early vegetables, all made possible by the wonderful climate. There are, in addition, large cattle ranches and sugar-cane and tobacco plantations. One of the most fertile farming areas is in the south, along the southern shore of Lake Okeechobee. All around the lake, however, are the Everglades, an untamed marshland of cypress and gum trees set among wide stretches of saw-grass, harbouring snakes, rare birds, alligators and a diminishing number of American crocodiles. Part of the Everglades is now being drained for cultivation but a large proportion of this fascinating region remains protected as a National Park.

As a holiday state, Florida has a great deal to offer. The focal point is Miami and its island city Miami Beach – the largest and most dazzling resort of all. Giant hotel and apartment blocks glint in the bright, reliable sunshine and are reflected in the warm, blue waters of Biscayne Bay and the Atlantic Ocean. Incredibly, these buildings that we see today were built on a wilderness of mangrove swamps, infested with mosquitoes and snakes.

With 1,500 miles of coastline and 800 miles of sandy beaches there is no shortage of resorts in Florida. North of Miami is exclusive Palm Beach – a city of wide boulevards and luxurious mansions – each with an enormous swimming pool set in exquisitely landscaped gardens.

Off the southern tip of Florida are the Florida Keys, a chain of delightful coral and limestone islands which number over 700, stretching far out into the Gulf of Mexico. Fifty of them are connected to each other and to the mainland by the remarkable Overseas Highway which crosses vast expanses of water, to end at Key West. This last island has a Caribbean atmosphere and was much favoured by past Presidents including Hoover, Franklin D. Roosevelt, Truman and Eisenhower. Without exception, however, all the Keys are excellent for the fishing and sailing facilities they can provide.

On Florida's west coast are two other important resorts, Tampa and St Petersburg – which is known as the 'sunshine city'. Besides being Florida's third largest city, Tampa is famous for its cigar industry which uses locally-grown tobacco. The capital of the state is Tallahassee, taken from an Indian phrase meaning 'old town'. Although it officially dates from 1824, another Spanish explorer, Ferdinando de Soto, discovered an Indian settlement on the site in 1529.

Orlando, which lies inland, is known as the 'city of lakes' and, indeed, more than fifty are within the city boundary. Orlando is close to one of Florida's most popular attractions, the spectacular Disneyworld. For children and adults alike the delights of this Magic Kingdom are endless and provide an unforgettable experience.

It is clear that one's choice of activity in Florida is far from limited. This all-year-round playground has facilities for sailing, fishing, snorkeling, scuba-diving, tennis and football, to name just a few. There are National Parks and Zoos to visit, old plantation houses, museums, Spanish missions and forts in which to capture the atmosphere of bygone days, white sand beaches to laze on and luxury hotels to be pampered in. Indeed, this southernmost state of the USA is certainly a land of plenty for both visitor and resident.

Left. An aerial view of Miami's famous coastline.

Key West, the southernmost city in the United States, lies 100 miles off the Florida coast. Although the island is relatively small, many tourists take advantage of its superb holiday facilities. It also accommodates one of the country's largest naval bases and the old colonial atmosphere is reflected in many of its houses, some beautiful examples of which can be seen on these pages.

Audubon House *top right* was built in 1830 for Captain John A. Geiger, who was a skilled pilot and master wrecker. The house was named after the famous naturalist and artist, John James Audubon, who was the Captain's guest in 1832. Many fine pieces of furniture can be seen in the interior which were collected from the many wrecks washed up along the Florida coast.

DEEP SEA FISHING
GULFSTREAM II
93.0 to 430. Capt. Tommy Lones FARE $12 00 Ph. 296-8494

Key West, the last island in the chain of approximately 700 islands which constitute the Florida Keys, owe their name to the Spanish word 'cayo'. The Sevenmile Bridge *centre right*, connects Key West with the Overseas Highway and also links a number of the keys.

Fishing is a favourite occupation at Key West and some of the well-equipped fishing boats can be seen *above and below right*.
Part of a day's catch of barracuda, watched by a thoughtful pelican *left* and *top near right* the excitement of a shark weigh-in.

Day over, the scene at sunset is transformed into a quiet and tranquil one *top far right*.

The Everglades National Park is a mysterious wilderness of mangrove swamps, cypress trees and sawgrass; the home of alligators, waterbirds and a few Seminole Indians. Alligators *left and below* closely resemble crocodiles in their general habits, swimming well with the aid of their powerful tails and feeding on fish and mammals.
The Anhinga Trail *right* is one way to view the alligators and birds in their natural habitat.

A Seminole village *below right* where the Indians try to preserve their traditional way of life. Of Greek origin, Seminole, signifies "runaway" and was given to the section of the Greek nation which emigrated in a body to Florida, where they live to the present day.

Overlooking Biscayne Bay on Miami's south shore is the gracious Viscaya – Dade County Art Museum *above*. This lovely Italian palazzo was built by James Deering to house a collection of Old World art.

To the south of Miami is the attractive town of Coral Gables built, incredibly, in the space of a year. The house *left* is typical of those in this area.

Miami's marina *right* takes on a magical quality when viewed at night.

As in other American cities skyscrapers are very much a part of the Miami skyline. Collins Avenue *left*, extending the length of Miami beach, is lined with apartment blocks and hotels, whilst *below*, yet more hotels line the waterfront.

Night falls on busy Miami Airport *centre left*.

Yachts and deep sea fishing boats lie becalmed in their moorings at Miami Marina *left*, and the towering skyscrapers are set against the lowering sky.

Two stunning night views of the Miami skyline *right*, seen from Biscayne Island.

Magic, modern Miami City with its vast complexes of cement, steel and glass is connected to the beach area by a number of causeways. The aerial views of Miami and its shoreline, pictured on these two pages, are truly impressive. Although now one of the most populous areas of the state, it is less than 100 years ago that the Tequesta Indians were in control of the backwoods lying to the west.

These aerial photographs well illustrate the natural conditions of water meeting land along a convoluted and fascinating shoreline. Left as they are, the bays, inlets and beaches provide a wide and excellent variety of opportunities for the enjoyment of water sports of all kinds. In many cases, however, artificial lakes and pools have been created, such as those at the famous Seaquarium *both pictures right*.

Visitors flock from all over the United States, as well as from places farther afield to enjoy the glorious sunshine for which Florida is so renowned. For many people this is enough but for those whose tastes run to more energetic pursuits there is always something to do. Golf courses abound and are deservedly popular.

One of Miami's most popular attractions is the world famous tropical oceanarium, aptly named Seaquarium. The photographs on these two pages show the killer whales performing a wide variety of tricks and each day many fascinating sea creatures including dolphins, sealions and fearsome sharks can also be seen during the continuous shows.

In the impressive and futuristic Seaquarium can be seen the seals *top far left corner*, whilst the friendly and gentle dolphins put on a spectacular show. These remarkable creatures are extremely intelligent and at the present time scientists are conducting a variety of experiments in the hope that communications between dolphins and humans might one day be possible.

Fifty years ago Miami Beach was a wilderness of mangrove swamps, infested with snakes and mosquitoes. Today it is the largest resort in the world attracting visitors from many countries eager to enjoy the luxury hotels, sub-tropical climate and fine beaches.

The clear turquoise water, white sandy beaches and dazzling hotels *overleaf* illustrate clearly the international appeal of this holiday playground.

These further outstanding aerial photographs clearly show the changing tones and colours of the waters that lap the shore of the ultra-modern resort of Miami. The colours change with the different light falling on them, from deep, intense greens to equally saturated blues. The water's hues show up the symmetry and careful planning of the clean, white hotels which seemingly fill every available pocket of space along the water's edge.

The obvious enjoyment of Miami's visitors as they swim in luxurious hotel swimming pools or play happily on the beach, is shown in the pictures on these two pages.

Colourful macaws fly freely through the naturally beautiful Parrot Jungle which is situated a few miles south of Miami. Giant cypress trees, oaks, orchids and bromeliads make it a fascinating place to visit.

A natural rain forest environment is enjoyed by these monkeys *right* which are the descendants of a small group that were imported from Singapore in 1933 and set free in what is now known as 'Monkey Jungle' as an experiment. The monkeys thrived in their new surroundings and soon multiplied to such an extent that there was a danger of them attacking intruders into 'their' territory and so a caged walkway was constructed to protect visitors.

Another inhabitant of the 'Monkey Jungle' is the elaborately dressed and bewigged chimpanzee *left* trained to entertain at hourly shows.

Snake handling is not an easily acquired accomplishment and, indeed, there are few people who would even wish to attempt such familiarity as is featured *below*.

Known as the Venice of America because of its extensive natural and artificial waterways. Fort Lauderdale is a popular winter resort for yachtsmen and fishermen alike. Sleek boats and lovely houses are a particular feature of the marina area. The city's deep water port at Port Everglades accommodates transatlantic liners and Caribbean cruise ships.

The unspoiled beauty of Birch State
Park, with its scenic railroad *top left*
is one of the highlights of Fort
Lauderdale. Spring fed lagoons and
ancient oaks are just two of the
many natural attractions to be
enjoyed here.

Hialeah Park *below and centre left*
is famous for its free flying flamingo
flock which is one of the largest in
captivity.

Boats once again dominate the
landscape at delightful Pompano
Beach *left* just north of Fort
Lauderdale

One of the greatest resorts in
Florida, Boca Raton *top right*, is
built mainly in a Spanish Gothic
style. It also boasts a fine 18 hole golf
course and beautiful ocean beach.

Situated between Pompano Beach
and Boca Raton is the tiny,
picturesque resort of Lighthouse
Point *right.*

Palm Beach, considered to be
Florida's most elegant and exclusive
resort, with wide palm fringed roads
below right, stylish shopping centres
below left and superb marina *above
left*, attracts countless visitors each
year.

Inland is the impressive Poinciana
Golf Club at Palm Springs *above
right*; its magnificent setting pure
delight to all golfers.

The awe inspiring rockets and
launch complex at the Kennedy
Space Centre *overleaf*.

Another spectacular marine life centre is Sea World, at Orlando in central Florida, featured *left*. Here in this aquatic wonderland can be seen, amongst others, killer whales, smiling dolphins, otters and penguins, where visitiors can also feed and touch some of these delightful creatures.

Possibly the greatest tourist attraction in the world is the incredible Disney World *right* which has undoubted appeal for the whole family.

The romantic spires of Cinderella's Castle soar into a perfect blue sky, *right, above and top left.*

The flowers *centre left* make a colourful splash but are they real?

A less tiring way of viewing at least part of Disney World is by the Mississippi riverboat, Richard E. Irvine, *below left,* whilst all the fun of the fair is available in this truly magical kingdom *below.*

At night Disney World takes on an even more magical quality and Cinderella's Castle *left*, enchanting against the black velvet sky, is a breathtaking sight for child and adult alike.

Looking down Main Street towards the castle *above*, the lights twinkle and glow in this most wonderful of wonderlands.

The dazzling fireworks display *right*, which is a prominent late night feature, fills the sky with vibrant colours as the firecrackers explode high over Cinderella's Castle.

Two of Walt Disney's most famous characters, Mickey Mouse and Donald Duck *left*.

The City Hall *above* makes an impressive sight and can be viewed from a horse-drawn trolley.

The old fire-engine *below* is yet another way of sightseeing or by riverboat *centre right*, which plies the extensive waterways.

A circular tour of the entire magic kingdom can be taken on an old-fashioned steam train *below far right*.

The fun and excitement of one of the many Main Street Parades, with all the best loved Disney characters *left*.

Rare film footage of the life and work of the famous film maker can be seen in the picturesque building *above*, whilst the delight of these young visitors *below* is obvious.

The perennial Disney favourites, Mickey, Donald and Pinnochio make a great trio *top far right*; the fire engine awaits its next batch of visitors *centre right* and *below far right* multi-coloured balloons festoon the square.

Ponce de Leon landed at St. Augustine on April 3rd 1513, claiming the country for Spain. It contains the oldest fort, built in 1672, in the U.S.A. and its other fine buildings include the Cordova Building Courthouse and Lightner Museum *above*, the Catholic Cathedral *left* and Flagler College *right*, all magnificent examples of Spanish inspired architecture.

Named in honour of General Andrew Jackson, who later became President, is the important industrial centre of Jacksonville *overleaf*, sited on the banks of the St. John's River. Of great importance industrially, many of the country's large insurance companies are also based here.

The capital city of the State of Florida is Tallahassee, meaning "old town". It contains many beautiful buildings, including plantation homes, mansions and churches dating back to pre-Civil War days. The lovely State Capital Building is pictured *below and centre left,* whilst the Holland Building, set in one of the many wide boulevards is featured *below left.*

East of Tallahassee is the Suwanee River *top left,* immortalized in the old folk melody by Stephen Foster, and popularised by the late Al Jolson. Its delightful setting makes it an ideal river for boating, particularly canoeing, and bathing.

Hollywood's replica of the "Bounty" in St. Petersburg Harbour *right* is enchanting when seen by night.

In the heart of Florida are the breathtaking Cypress Gardens *left*, where spectacular blooms can be seen all year round. It houses many tropical plants and blossoms which visitors may see along the winding waterways by taking one of the unique electric boat tours. The towering cypress trees, and the evening sun glinting through the leaves, make a beautiful picture as they line the shimmering water's edge of Lake Eloise *right*. The giant fig tree *below right*, like an enormous umbrella, never fails to amaze visitors to these fantastic gardens.

On Florida's East Coast, are the exotic Busch Gardens *below*, known as the "Dark Continent of Tampa". The flamingoes *below* are just one of the 1500 species of birds which are to be found in this most unusual of gardens where rhinos, zebras, lions and giraffes all roam free in their own 200 acre preserve.

The sunshine skyway over Tampa Bay whose bridge *above left*, is reputed to be 15 storeys high. An old steam locomotive at Bradenton *far left*. *Near left*, surrounded by palm trees, stands the First Presbyterian Church. With fine views over the bay is Sarasota *top right*, below which can be seen the Pier Restaurant and Marina at Bradenton. This unusual modern building dominates the pier at St. Petersburg *below right*, above which can be seen the fishing boats moored at Caloosamatchee River Bridge, Fort Myers.

In the town of Naples, S.W. Florida, the Venetian villas *overleaf* overlook the Gulf of Mexico.

First published in Great Britain 1978 by Colour Library International Ltd.
© Illustrations: Colour Library International Ltd. Colour separations by La Cromolito, Milan, Italy.
Display and text filmsetting by Focus Photoset, London, England.
Printed and bound by SAGDOS - Brugherio (MI), Italy.
Published by Crescent Books, a division of Crown Publishers Inc.
Library of Congress Catalogue Card No. 78-59844
CRESCENT 1978